Hedging market risk in optimal liquidation

Phillip Monin*

November 13, 2014

Abstract

Financial institutions commonly face the risk that large trades will execute at unfavorable prices due to price impact effects from insufficient market liquidity. A typical method to manage these price impact effects is to split a given order into smaller pieces and to trade these pieces sequentially over time. Such a strategy, however, is exposed to market risk. Unlike price impact, market risk can be hedged. This paper explores the market risk management of the liquidation of a large trade that is subject to price impact. Specifically, we consider an investor, such as a large financial institution or a broker-dealer, who must *a priori* liquidate a large position in a *primary* risky asset whose price is influenced by the investor's liquidation strategy. The investor hedges the market risk involved with liquidation by simultaneously taking a position in a liquid *proxy* asset that is imperfectly correlated with the primary asset. We show that the optimal strategies for an investor with a finite investment horizon and constant absolute risk aversion are deterministic and we find them explicitly using the calculus of variations. We find that the liquidation strategy for an investor able to hedge market risk is the same as the liquidation strategy of a less risk-averse investor without such a hedge. Similarly, the liquidation strategy for an investor able to hedge market risk is the same as for an investor facing higher price impact effects but without the ability to hedge market risk.

Keywords: optimal liquidation, optimal execution, hedging market risk, block trades, indifference price, price spread

---

*phillip.monin@treasury.gov; Office of Financial Research, U.S. Department of the Treasury. 717 14th St NW, Washington, DC 20005. The author would like to thank Thaleia Zariphopoulou, Rick Bookstaber, Mihai Sîrbu, Gordan Žitković, Benjamin Kay, an anonymous referee, seminar participants at the Office of Financial Research and the University of Texas at Austin, and conference participants at the Sixth Western Conference in Mathematical Finance for their valuable suggestions. The author would also like to thank the Oxford-Man Institute for its hospitality and support of a long-term visit during which most of this work was completed.

1 Introduction

Large financial institutions commonly face the problem of how to efficiently liquidate large blocks of shares. Examples include large asset managers who sell assets to meet redemptions or to rebalance portfolios, insurance companies who sell holdings to pay claims, and private equity firms who sell stakes in portfolio companies after taking them public. Instantaneous execution of a block of shares that constitutes a significant percentage of the average daily volume of a stock might either be impossible or prohibitively expensive due to a lack of sufficient market liquidity. An institution might attempt to solve this problem by splitting its large order into smaller blocks and trading these blocks sequentially over time. If the institution seeks but cannot find instant liquidity, however, then it essentially has two options: trade in a so-called dark pool or solicit the services of a broker-dealer. The broker-dealer may execute the institution's trade on an agency basis or on a principal basis in a so-called bought deal. If the broker-dealer trades as principal with the financial institution in a bought deal, it provides the instant liquidity that the institution demands by assuming ownership of its entire position in exchange for compensation. The broker-dealer will then typically form a syndicate of buyers for subsets of the original block of shares, with any residual remaining in its inventory. This residual inventory is generally liquidated over time and is thus subject to market risk, which can be at least partially hedged by taking a symmetric position in a related and relatively liquid asset. For example, if the residual inventory to be liquidated is 1,500,000 shares of stock in Procter & Gamble, the broker-dealer might immediately take a short position in the S&P 500 Index using, perhaps, index futures contracts or exchange traded funds tracking the index. Over time, the broker-dealer sells its long position in Procter & Gamble and buys back its short position in the S&P 500 Index. The returns of Procter & Gamble and the S&P 500 are likely correlated, and being long one and short the other partially reduces the market risk on the overall position.

In this paper, we study the problem faced by an investor who must balance the need to liquidate with the costs of illiquidity. Specifically, we consider the problem faced by an investor who must *a priori* liquidate a large position in a *primary* risky asset whose price is influenced by the investor's strategy. The investor attempts to hedge the market risk involved in liquidating over time by simultaneously taking a position in a liquid *proxy* risky asset that is imperfectly correlated with the primary asset. The investor is assumed to be either a large financial institution or a broker-dealer trading as principal in a block trade.

Liquidation is assumed to be motivated purely by exogenous liquidity reasons, e.g. portfolio rebalancing, cash flow, or hedging. The investor is not motivated by private information about the fundamental value of the assets.

It is assumed that the investor's trades in the primary asset impact its price due to adverse feedback effects from the sizes of the trades. Conversely, the proxy asset is taken to be perfectly liquid. The price of the primary asset is modeled as an instance of the Almgren-Chriss model for price impact (see Almgren and Chriss (1999), Almgren and Chriss (2001), and Almgren (2003)), while the price of the proxy asset is modeled according to a Bachelier model with drift. Market risk is proxied by the covariance matrix of the two assets. Proceeds from the liquidation of the primary asset are deposited into a riskless money market account, and the investor then uses these funds to take positions in the liquid proxy asset. Liquidation must be completed by a prespecified terminal time. Following Schöneborn (2008), Schied and Schöneborn (2009), and Schied et al. (2010), among others, we assume that the investor's criterion is to maximize his expected utility of terminal wealth. Herein, we assume that the investor's the utility function exhibits constant absolute risk aversion (CARA).

Our results are as follows. We use an extension of a technique found in Schied et al. (2010) to show that the optimal strategies for the CARA investor are deterministic functions of time. We find closed-form expressions for the optimal strategies using calculus of variations and analyze their properties. We also compute the broker-dealer's minimum fee for entering into an agreement to trade as principal with a liquidity-demanding financial institution.

In turn, we restrict our attention to the no-drift market, where we show several interesting properties of the optimal liquidation strategies. We show that, as the correlation between the primary and proxy assets approaches one, the investor increasingly acts as if he were risk-neutral. More generally, we establish that an increase in the correlation between the proxy and the primary assets has the effect that the investor liquidates his position in the primary asset as if he were less risk-averse (holding all else constant). Similarly, an increase in the correlation between the proxy and the primary asset has the effect that the investor liquidates as if there were less price impact (holding all else constant). Finally, we show that the investor is always better off, in terms of his expected utility, by hedging the market risk involved with liquidation using a correlated and relatively liquid proxy asset.

Market risk management for a risk-averse investor facing price impact risk because of a need to liquidate a large position has not been studied from a theoretical normative perspective. The most closely related paper to ours is Ankirchner et al. (2013), who study the trade-off facing a risk-neutral investor between paying for instant liquidity to hedge a forward position and the basis risk involved in hedging it with futures contracts. Also, Rogers and Singh (2010) and Li and Almgren (2014) study the effects of illiquidity costs on the hedging strategies of European claims.

Broadly speaking, the literature on price impact and block trades tends to focus on a few separate but related objectives. These objectives include understanding the market microstructure foundations of price impact and understanding the activities and optimal liquidation strategies of the large trader. Empirical studies of the price effects of large trades (see, among others, Kraus and Stoll (1972), Holthausen et al. (1987), Stoll (1989), Holthausen et al. (1990), Keim and Madhavan (1995a), Keim and Madhavan (1995b), Almgren et al. (2005), Frino et al. (2006), Obizhaeva (2007), and Ryu (2013)) have demonstrated that the size of the trade adversely influences the price at which it is executed and that prices following a large trade only partially recover to their ex-ante levels. Several explanations for these effects are put forth in the literature. Kyle (1985) and Easley and O'Hara (1987), for example, provide theoretical frameworks in which these price effects are explained by the existence of asymmetric information among investors. On the other hand, price effects in Grossman and Miller (1988) arise because liquidity demanders effectively pay other market participants to hold suboptimal portfolios for the privilege of transacting sooner rather than later.

A separate line of literature, beginning with Bertsimas and Lo (1998) and Almgren and Chriss (1999), take these empirical price effects as exogenous instead of attempting to explain them. For recent developments see, among others, Obizhaeva and Wang (2013), Schied and Schöneborn (2009), Gatheral and Schied (2011), Predoiu et al. (2011), Schied (2013), Li and Almgren (2014) and Bechler and Ludkovski (2014). The treatment of price effects as exogenous typically results in analytically tractable statistical models that can be used to study the optimal liquidation strategies for large trades. Herein, we focus on this latter segment of the literature in our study of the optimal liquidation and hedging strategies of the investor. Aside from tractability, we base our model on a continuous-time version of the model introduced by Bertsimas and Lo (1998) and Almgren and Chriss (1999) (see, among others, Almgren (2003)) because it forms the basis for many liquidation algorithms used in practice and because the model separates the effects of market risk and price impact risk, which is germane to our objective.

The problem we pose is consistent with theoretical results from the literature. For example, Burdett and O'Hara (1987) consider the syndication strategy of a block trader and demonstrate that it is optimal for a block trader to retain a position in the asset due to search costs. In addition, Seppi (1990) shows that a large trader who trades solely for portfolio rebalancing reasons, rather than for information-related reasons, chooses to trade in off-exchange alternative trading mechanisms, such as dark pools and block trading services, rather than liquidate over time on an exchange. Finally, this paper is also related to the literature on dealers' inventory management. Stoll (1978) shows that the dealer's price to provide liquidity is related to the compensation he requires to hold a suboptimal portfolio position, and that this price is thus increasing in his risk aversion. In a model integrating a bank's risk management and capital structure and budgeting decisions, Froot and Stein (1998) argue that a broker-dealer commands a risk premium for exposure to non-hedgeable risks and that this risk premium is based on correlations with the broker-dealer's existing inventory of non-hedgeable risks.

The paper is organized as follows. In section 2, we present the continuous-time model and derive the value of the investor's portfolio through time. In section 3, we show that the optimal strategies are deterministic and we construct them explicitly. We then analyze the optimal strategies and compute the broker-dealer's minimum fee for transacting in a bought deal. In section 4, we restrict our attention to the no-drift market. We conclude in section 5. For the reader's convenience, we provide all proofs in an appendix.

2 The market environment

We describe the market environment in which the investor operates. The investor starts at time $t = 0$ and must liquidate a large position in a risky asset, called the *primary* asset, by an exogenous terminal time $T > 0$. Liquidation proceeds are deposited into a riskless money market account that pays zero interest. The money market account is paired with a perfectly liquid risky asset, called the *proxy* asset, to form a portfolio that the investor rebalances over time. The primary asset has price S_t^I, $0 \leq t \leq T$, and exhibits price impact due to the feedback effects of the investor's liquidation strategy. Its price dynamics follow a simple Almgren-Chriss model (see Almgren and Chriss (1999, 2001) and Almgren (2003)). Therefore, the price admits a decomposition into the sum of a so-called unaffected component and a price impact component. Namely,

$$S_t^I = \widetilde{S}_t^I + I_t, \tag{1}$$

where the unaffected component, $\widetilde{S}_t^I$, corresponds to the price available in the market if the investor were not trading, and the price impact component, I_t, represents the per-share cost that the investor incurs in order to liquidate his position.

The price of the unaffected component, $\widetilde{S}_t^I, 0 \leq t \leq T$, of the primary asset and the price of the proxy asset, $S_t, 0 \leq t \leq T$, are both given by Bachelier models with drift. Specifically,

$$\widetilde{S}_t^I = S_0^I + \mu_I t + \sigma_I W_t^I \tag{2}$$

and

$$S_t = S_0 + \mu t + \sigma W_t, \tag{3}$$

where $S_0^I, S_0, \mu_I, \sigma_I, \mu$ and σ are positive constants, and W_t^I and W_t, $0 \leq t \leq T$, are standard, correlated Brownian motions, with correlation coefficient

$$\rho \in [0, 1), \tag{4}$$

defined on a filtered probability space $(\Omega, \mathcal{F}, (\mathcal{F}_t), \mathbb{P})$ in which the filtration $(\mathcal{F}_t)$, $0 \leq t \leq T$, satisfies the usual conditions of completeness and right-continuity.

We note that μ_I and μ are absolute (not percentage) mean returns and, respectively, σ_I and σ are absolute (not percentage) volatilities. Market risk in this environment is proxied by the covariance matrix

$$\Sigma = \begin{pmatrix} \sigma^2 & \rho\sigma\sigma_I \\ \rho\sigma\sigma_I & \sigma_I^2 \end{pmatrix}.$$

The above assumptions on the drifts and entries of the covariance matrix guarantee the absence of arbitrage opportunities between the unaffected component (2) of the primary asset and the proxy asset (3).

Let η_t, $0 \leq t \leq T$, denote the number of shares that the investor holds in the primary asset. We assume that the investor is initially long the primary asset, i.e.

$\eta_0 > 0$, and require that liquidation is complete at terminal time, i.e. $\eta_T = 0$. We further assume that the mapping $t \mapsto \eta_t$ is absolutely continuous with derivative $\dot{\eta}_t$.

The price impact component I_t of the primary asset (1) admits the decomposition

$$I_t = \gamma(\eta_t - \eta_0) + \theta\dot{\eta}_t,$$

where $\gamma \geq 0$ is called the coefficient of permanent price impact and $\theta > 0$ is called the coefficient of temporary price impact. For information on estimating the coefficients of permanent and temporary price impact see, among others, Almgren and Chriss (1999) and Almgren et al. (2005). We deduce from (1) and (2) that the price of the primary asset can be written as

$$S_t^I = S_0^I + \mu_I t + \sigma_I W_t^I + \gamma(\eta_t - \eta_0) - \theta\xi_t, \tag{5}$$

where we have represented $\dot{\eta}_t$ by $-\xi_t$, so that

$$\eta_t = \eta_0 - \int_0^t \xi_u du, \qquad 0 \leq t \leq T. \tag{6}$$

We use π_t, $0 \leq t \leq T$, to denote the number of shares of the proxy asset that the investor holds. We assume that the process $\pi = (\pi_t)$ is self-financing. Moreover, we assume that the process (π_t, ξ_t), $0 \leq t \leq T$, is $\mathcal{F}_t$-progressively measurable and that $|\pi_t|$ and $|\xi_t|$ are bounded uniformly for almost all (t, ω). We denote by $\mathcal{A}(T, \eta_0)$ the set of processes (π_t, ξ_t), $0 \leq t \leq T$, that satisfy the above assumptions and the so-called finite fuel constraint, namely

$$\eta_0 = \int_0^T \xi_u du.$$

In turn, we denote by $\mathcal{A}_{\text{det}}(T, \eta_0)$ the subset of *deterministic* processes in $\mathcal{A}(T, \eta_0)$.

The above model for the price S_t^I, $0 \leq t \leq T$, of the primary asset is frequently called the Almgren-Chriss model of price impact, named for the authors of the foundational papers Almgren and Chriss (1999) and Almgren and Chriss (2001) (see, also, Almgren (2003)), although versions of the model appeared earlier (see, for example, Bertsimas and Lo (1998) and Madhavan (2000)). The Almgren-Chriss model incorporates both the permanent and temporary price impacts observed in empirical studies of large trades (see, among others, Kraus and Stoll (1972), Holthausen et al. (1987), Stoll (1989), Holthausen et al. (1990), Keim and Madhavan (1995a), Keim and Madhavan (1995b), Almgren et al. (2005), Frino et al. (2006), Obizhaeva (2007) and Ryu (2013)) while also being sufficiently tractable for the analysis of optimal trading strategies.

A shortcoming of the model is that the prices of the primary and proxy assets can become negative. For instance, the price of the proxy may become negative with probability

$$\mathbb{P}(S_t < 0) = \mathbb{P}(S_0 + \mu t + \sigma W_t < 0) = \Phi\left(-\frac{(S_0 + \mu t)}{\sigma\sqrt{t}}\right),$$

where Φ is the cumulative distribution function of the standard normal random variable. However, even very large asset positions are typically liquidated within a few days or hours, and it is reasonable to assume that $S_0 + \mu t$ is much larger than $\sigma\sqrt{t}$ and that, in turn, the price of the proxy becomes negative only with negligible probability.

A similar remark holds for the price of the primary asset, although this price may also become negative because of the temporary and permanent price components in (5). This may happen, for instance, when a very large asset position is sold in a very short time interval. With realistic parameter values, however, negative prices for the primary asset will occur with only negligible probability.

We stress that since the investor is selling a position in the primary asset, we expect that the path of η_t, $0 \leq t \leq T$, will be non-increasing and, in turn, of finite variation. Therefore, assuming that the mapping $t \mapsto \eta_t$ is absolutely continuous is reasonable. We could allow for jumps in η_t, but this leads to analytical intractability. Moreover, in a model allowing jumps, Obizhaeva and Wang (2013) find that, for realistic model parameters, the optimal strategy is absolutely continuous except for very small trades at the front and back ends of the trading horizon.

2.1 Portfolio value

We derive the value of the investor's portfolio that consists of positions in the proxy asset and the riskless money market into which liquidation proceeds from the primary asset are deposited. Over the horizon $[0, T]$, the investor liquidates the long position in the primary asset into a riskless money market account that pays zero interest and initially has zero balance.[1] At time t, the investor sells $\xi_t dt = -\dot{\eta}_t dt$ shares of the primary asset for price S_t^I. The value of the money market account, $V_t(\xi)$, $0 \leq t \leq T$, following strategy $\xi = (\xi_t)$ is therefore $\int_0^t \xi_s S_s^I ds$. Using (5) and integrating by parts, we obtain that $V_t(\xi)$ can be written as

$$V_t(\xi) = S_0^I \eta_0 - \frac{\gamma}{2}\eta_0^2 + \mu_I \int_0^t \eta_s ds + \sigma_I \int_0^t \eta_s dW_s^I - \theta \int_0^t \xi_s^2 ds$$
$$- \eta_t \left(S_0^I + \mu_I t + \sigma_I W_t^I + \frac{\gamma}{2}(\eta_t - 2\eta_0) \right),$$

where η_t, $0 \leq t \leq T$, is given by (6).

The investor then trades between the money market account and the liquid proxy asset in a self-financing fashion. The position in the proxy is worth $\pi_t S_t$ at time t, and the self-financing assumption implies $d(\pi_t S_t) = \pi_t dS_t$. Therefore, the total

---

[1] The zero initial balance in the money market account means that we assume that the investor has zero initial wealth. Mathematically this assumption is innocuous, as the optimal strategy for a CARA utility function is independent of initial wealth (see Theorem 3.1). However, from a practical perspective this assumption is undesirable, as one expects in reality that the investor's initial capital will affect his risk-bearing capacity and consequently his optimal strategies.

value of the investor's portfolio, $X = X_t^{\pi,\xi}$, $0 \leq t \leq T$, is given by

$$\begin{aligned}
X_t^{\pi,\xi} &= V_t(\xi) + \int_0^t \pi_s dS_s \\
&= x_0 + \mu_I \int_0^t \eta_s ds + \sigma_I \int_0^t \eta_s dW_s^I - \theta \int_0^t \xi_s^2 ds + \mu \int_0^t \pi_s ds \\
&\quad + \sigma \int_0^t \pi_s dW_s - \eta_t \left(S_0^I + \mu_I t + \sigma_I W_t^I + \frac{\gamma}{2}(\eta_t - 2\eta_0) \right),
\end{aligned}$$

where the constant x_0 is defined as

$$x_0 = S_0^I \eta_0 - \frac{\gamma}{2}\eta_0^2. \tag{7}$$

Finally, the condition $\eta_T = 0$ implies that the value of the portfolio at terminal time T can be written as

$$X_T^{\pi,\xi} = x_0 + \mu_I \int_0^T \eta_s ds + \sigma_I \int_0^T \eta_s dW_s^I - \theta \int_0^T \xi_s^2 ds + \mu \int_0^T \pi_s ds + \sigma \int_0^T \pi_s dW_s. \tag{8}$$

2.2 Regularity considerations

Standard financial models are considered regular or viable if they do not admit arbitrage opportunities. However, Huberman and Stanzl (2004) were among the first to identify additional irregularities that can occur in price impact models which can lead to the non-existence of optimal strategies. Other notions of market irregularity in price impact models have since been introduced and studied by Klöck et al. (2011), Gatheral and Schied (2011), Alfonsi et al. (2012), Roch and Soner (2013), among others. We now briefly discuss these notions of irregularity and comment on the regularity of our model.

To distinguish between the effects of price impact and the effects from potentially profitable strategies arising from exploiting the drift, regularity conditions are formulated in the no-drift setting, i.e. where $\mu = \mu_I = 0$. Moreover, the regularity conditions are formed in terms of the expected value of liquidation proceeds. There are three related, but not necessarily equivalent, notions of regularity that are popular in the optimal execution literature. These are: the absence of price manipulation, the absence of transaction-triggered price manipulation, and the absence of negative expected execution costs (see Gatheral and Schied (2011) for a review).

In our setting, a price manipulation strategy is a policy (π, ξ), with corresponding position η in the primary asset given by (6), that satisfies $\eta_0 = \eta_T = 0$ and is such that $\mathbb{E}(X_T^{\pi,\xi}) > 0$. Such strategies were introduced by Huberman and Stanzl (2004). Therein, it was shown that, in some models, the presence of price manipulation strategies can lead to "quasi-arbitrage," which is a weak form of arbitrage. Moreover, in our setting, the existence of price manipulation would imply the non-existence of an optimal execution strategy for a risk-neutral investor. This is because an arbitrarily large expected terminal wealth can be generated by a strategy that adds together multiples of a price manipulation strategy (see Klöck et al. (2011)). Although the absence of price manipulation strategies is necessary for the regularity of price impact models, Alfonsi et al. (2012) observe that it is not sufficient. Therein, the authors propose the notion of transaction-triggered price manipulation, which occurs if the expected revenues of a liquidation order can be increased by intermediate buy trades. In our setting, transaction-triggered price manipulation occurs if there exists an initial position η_0, a liquidation horizon $T > 0$, and a corresponding strategy $(\bar{\pi}, \bar{\xi}) = (\bar{\pi}, \bar{\xi})(\eta_0, T)$ such that $\mathbb{E}(X_T^{\bar{\pi}, \bar{\xi}})$ is strictly greater than the supremum of $\mathbb{E}(X_T^{\pi, \xi})$ over all strategies $(\pi, \xi) = (\pi, \xi)(\eta_0, T)$ that are monotone increasing or decreasing in time. Finally, the third notion of irregularity, called negative expected execution costs, was introduced independently by Klöck et al. (2011) and Roch and Soner (2013). In our setting, the market admits negative expected execution costs if there exists a liquidation horizon $T > 0$ and a corresponding liquidation strategy $(\pi, \xi) = (\pi, \xi)(T)$ such that $\mathbb{E}(X_T^{\pi, \xi}) > \eta_0 S_0^I$. For the relations among the above notions of irregularity in price impact models, we refer the reader to Klöck et al. (2011).

We now comment on the regularity of our model. In our setting, the expected value of the portfolio at terminal time (in the no-drift market) is given by

$$\mathbb{E}(X_T^{\pi, \xi}) = x_0 - \theta \int_0^T \xi_s^2 ds. \qquad (9)$$

A straightforward application of Jensen's inequality and the strict concavity of the mapping $(\pi, \xi) \mapsto \mathbb{E}(X_T^{\pi, \xi})$ shows that the unique liquidation strategy ξ_t^* that maximizes the expected revenues (9) among admissible strategies $(\pi, \xi) \in \mathcal{A}(T, \eta_0)$ has constant trading rate, namely

$$\xi_t^* = \frac{\eta_0}{T}. \qquad (10)$$

We note that in practice time is usually parameterized in volume time, and for this reason, (10) is commonly called a volume-weighted average price (VWAP) strategy. The significance of finding the explicit solution (10) to the problem of maximizing liquidation revenues is that it can be combined with the results of Klöck et al. (2011) to deduce that the model herein is free from price manipulation, transaction-triggered price manipulation, and negative expected execution costs.

3 Solution under CARA risk preferences

We pose and solve the investor's optimization problem. The investor faces a trade-off between the costs of quick liquidation and market risk exposure in slow liquidation. Following Schied and Schöneborn (2009) and Schied et al. (2010), among others, we assume that the investor is risk-averse and seeks to maximize the expected utility of the terminal value of his wealth.

We assume that the investor's utility function u is of the exponential (CARA) form,
$$u(x) = -e^{-\alpha x}, \tag{11}$$
where $\alpha > 0$ is the absolute risk aversion coefficient. In turn, the investor's objective is to solve
$$v(T, x_0, \eta_0) = \sup_{(\pi,\xi) \in \mathcal{A}(T,\eta_0)} \mathbb{E}\left(-\exp(-\alpha X_T^{\pi,\xi})\right), \tag{12}$$
where x_0 is given by (7), $X_T^{\pi,\xi}$ is as in (8), $\eta_0 > 0$ is the initial position in the primary asset, and the set $\mathcal{A}(T, \eta_0)$ in defined in section 2.

A natural conjecture is that the optimal strategies solving (12) are deterministic. To see why, consider that in the original Merton problem (see Merton (1969)), the optimal investment policy for a CARA investor in a market in which the price of the risky asset is given by a Bachelier model with drift is to hold a constant number of shares in the risky asset through time. Moreover, as Schied et al. (2010) show, the optimal liquidation strategy for a CARA investor in a pure liquidation model (without the proxy asset) is deterministic. The following theorem shows that this conjecture is indeed valid.

Theorem 3.1. *Let the positive constant κ_ρ be defined by*
$$\kappa_\rho := \sqrt{\frac{\alpha \sigma_I^2 (1-\rho^2)}{2\theta}}, \tag{13}$$
where ρ is as in (4), σ_I and θ as in (5), and α as in (11). Then, the a.s-unique optimal policy in (12) is the deterministic strategy (π^*, ξ^*) given by
$$\pi_t^* = \frac{1}{\alpha} \frac{\mu}{\sigma^2} - \rho \frac{\sigma_I}{\sigma} \eta_t^*, \tag{14}$$
and
$$\xi_t^* = \kappa_\rho \eta_0 \frac{\cosh(\kappa_\rho(T-t))}{\sinh(\kappa_\rho T)} + \left(\rho \frac{\mu}{\sigma} - \frac{\mu_I}{\sigma_I}\right) \frac{e^{\kappa_\rho(T-t)} - e^{\kappa_\rho t}}{\sqrt{2\alpha\theta(1-\rho^2)}(e^{\kappa_\rho T}+1)}, \tag{15}$$
where
$$\eta_t^* = \eta_0 \frac{\sinh(\kappa_\rho(T-t))}{\sinh(\kappa_\rho T)} - \left(\rho \frac{\mu}{\sigma} - \frac{\mu_I}{\sigma_I}\right) \frac{(e^{\kappa_\rho(T-t)} - 1)(e^{\kappa_\rho t} - 1)}{\alpha(1-\rho^2)\sigma_I(e^{\kappa_\rho T}+1)}. \tag{16}$$

The optimal allocation π^* in the proxy asset in (14) is the sum of the myopic Merton portfolio for optimal investment in the proxy asset (see Merton (1969)) and a hedging demand component given in terms of the position in the primary asset. This hedging demand is always negative, as the investor hedges the market risk involved in the liquidation by shorting a specific number of shares of the proxy asset, and then rebalancing dynamically over time as the shares in the primary asset are liquidated. The number of shares is given by the so-called minimum variance hedge ratio, $\rho\sigma_I/\sigma$. Note that a similar result appears in Ankirchner et al. (2013). Furthermore, observe that the hedge ratio can be estimated empirically as the beta of a regression of prices of the primary asset on prices of the proxy asset.[2]

As the optimal strategies (14), (15) and (16) are deterministic functions of time, we observe that under CARA preferences there is no intertemporal updating over the liquidation horizon. This aspect also holds in the pure liquidation setting in more general optimal execution models (see, for example, Schied et al. (2010)) and in many algorithms in practice.

If $\rho = 0$ then the optimal strategies in the primary and proxy assets decouple. That is,

$$\pi_t^* = \frac{1}{\alpha}\frac{\mu}{\sigma^2}, \qquad \eta_t^* = \eta_0 \frac{\sinh(\kappa_0(T-t))}{\sinh(\kappa T)} + \frac{\mu_I}{\sigma_I}\frac{(e^{\kappa_0(T-t)}-1)(e^{\kappa_0 t}-1)}{\alpha\sigma_I(e^{\kappa_0 T}+1)},$$

where $\kappa_0 = \sqrt{\frac{\alpha\sigma_I^2}{2\theta}}$. These are, respectively, the optimal strategies for the Merton problem under CARA preferences (see Merton (1969)) and the optimal strategies for pure liquidation problem of an asset with price impact in a market without a proxy (see Schied et al. (2010)).

The correlation-adjusted difference in the Sharpe ratios of the assets,

$$\rho\frac{\mu}{\sigma} - \frac{\mu_I}{\sigma_I}, \qquad (17)$$

appears in the second components of both (15) and (16). This quantity represents the extent to which directional or trend views in the primary and proxy assets enter into the liquidation strategies, since it is the only place that the drifts μ_I and μ of the primary and proxy assets appear in the optimal strategies for the primary asset. Thus, both the speed of liquidation and the number of shares in the primary asset can be decomposed into the sum of the no-drift solution (see section 4) and a term incorporating drift effects. A similar decomposition appeared in Almgren and Chriss (1999) and Schied et al. (2010). The second term incorporating drift effects allows the investor to adjust his speed of liquidation in order to take advantage of his directional views on the assets.

Finally, the proof of Theorem 3.1 shows (see (33) in the appendix) that the maximal terminal expected utility (12) can be written in terms of ξ^* and η^* alone, i.e. in terms of only the optimal strategies for the primary asset. Specifically,

$$\mathbb{E}[u(X_T^{\pi^*,\xi^*})] = -\exp\left(-\alpha S_0^I \eta_0 + \alpha\frac{\gamma}{2}\eta_0^2 - \frac{1}{2}\frac{\mu^2}{\sigma^2}T + \alpha\theta\int_0^T (\xi_t^*)^2 dt \right.$$
$$\left. -\alpha\mu_I(1-\rho)\int_0^T \eta_t^* dt + \frac{\alpha^2}{2}(1-\rho^2)\sigma_I^2\int_0^T (\eta_t^*)^2 dt\right). \qquad (18)$$

---

[2]Recall that, for tractability, prices in the model are given by arithmetic Brownian motions with drift, not by geometric Brownian motions as is typically assumed. Therefore, the proposed regression uses time series of price data and not returns data.

3.1 The broker-dealer's minimum fee or discount

One way that financial institutions can obtain instant liquidity is by entering into an agreement with a broker-dealer in which the broker-dealer agrees to trade as principal with the institution in exchange for an upfront fee. Such a fee is frequently quoted as a spread or on a discount basis. We now compute the minimum fee that the broker-dealer should charge a liquidity-demanding financial institution to enter into such an agreement. At time $t = 0$, this fee is defined by the amount $h(\eta_0, T)$ such that the broker-dealer is indifferent between (i) not trading at all, and (ii) agreeing to trade as principal with the institution, and then investing optimally while taking into account, on the one hand, the liability of liquidating the shares in the primary asset with price impact, and on the other, the compensation $h(\eta_0, T)$. Therefore, in a financial economics context, the broker-dealer's minimum fee can be interpreted as his indifference price for taking on and liquidating the financial institution's position.

Proposition 3.2. *Let ξ^* and η^* be given by (15) and (16), respectively. The broker-dealer's minimum fee $h(\eta_0, T)$ at time $t = 0$ for trading as principal with a liquidity-demanding financial institution is given by*

$$h(\eta_0, T) = \frac{\gamma}{2}\eta_0^2 + \theta \int_0^T (\xi_t^*)^2 dt + \frac{\alpha}{2}(1-\rho^2)\sigma_I^2 \int_0^T (\eta_t^*)^2 dt \qquad (19)$$

$$- \left(S_0^I \eta_0 + \frac{1}{2\alpha}\frac{\mu^2}{\sigma^2}T + \mu_I(1-\rho) \int_0^T \eta_t^* dt \right). \qquad (20)$$

The various components of the broker-dealer's minimum fee admit the following economic interpretation. The first term in (19) shows that the effect of the permanent price impact γ enters only through the initial position η_0 in the primary asset and is unaffected by the presence of the proxy as a hedge. The second term in (19) accounts for the temporary price impact over the liquidation period through the temporary impact coefficient θ and an integral of the square of the speed of liquidation that, in effect, represents the nonlinear nature of the transactions costs involved. The third integral in (19) incorporates the volatility risk involved in the transaction. These terms are all positive and thus are factors that increase the indifference price. As seen in (20), three other positive terms are then subtracted, and therefore are factors that decrease the indifference price. The first term in (20) is the book value of the shares of the primary asset. In the case of the broker-dealer accepting to trade as principal with another institution, this is the book value of the shares that are transferred to the broker-dealer for liquidation. The last two terms in (20) represent the positive value of exploiting the drifts of the two assets in the course of liquidation.

4 Liquidation in the no-drift market

We consider the special case of liquidating in a no-drift market environment, by which we mean that $\mu = \mu_I = 0$. This corresponds to the case where the prices of the proxy asset and the unaffected component of the primary asset are martingales. In other words, the investor does not have directional views on the future prices of the assets. Martingality of the unaffected component of the asset under liquidation is commonly assumed in the optimal execution literature on the basis that drift effects can largely be ignored due to short trading horizons (see, among others, Almgren and Chriss (1999), Almgren (2003), and Klöck et al. (2011)).

From Theorem 3.1, the optimal strategies in the no-drift market are given by

$$\pi_t^* = -\rho \frac{\sigma_I}{\sigma} \eta_t^*, \tag{21}$$

$$\xi_t^* = \kappa_\rho \eta_0 \frac{\cosh(\kappa_\rho(T-t))}{\sinh(\kappa_\rho T)}, \tag{22}$$

and

$$\eta_t^* = \eta_0 \frac{\sinh(\kappa_\rho(T-t))}{\sinh(\kappa_\rho T)}, \tag{23}$$

where we recall that κ_ρ is given by

$$\kappa_\rho := \sqrt{\frac{\alpha \sigma_I^2 (1-\rho^2)}{2\theta}}. \tag{24}$$

Figures 1, 2 and 3 describe the optimal strategies in the no-drift market for varying levels of the correlation ρ between the unaffected component of the primary asset and the proxy. The correlation ρ represents the effect of the proxy asset on hedging the market risk involved in liquidating the primary asset over time.

The policy ξ^*, the optimal speed of liquidating the primary asset, is shown in Figure 1. The strategy has steepest gradient and is most convex when there is no correlation, and both its gradient and curvature decrease as ρ increases. As the correlation between the primary and proxy assets increases and the market risk is increasingly hedged, the investor becomes less "impatient" in his need to liquidate his position in the primary asset.

Figure 2 depicts the optimal number of shares in the proxy asset through time. If the correlation is zero, then the Merton strategy is optimal. On the other hand, if the correlation is positive, the optimal strategy is to immediately short a certain number of shares given by the hedge ratio $\rho \sigma_I / \sigma$ and then to gradually buy back the shares over time. This is the mechanism by which the market risk involved in liquidating the primary asset over time is hedged by the presence of the correlated proxy asset.

Figure 3 shows the optimal allocation in the primary asset through time. The strategy is most convex when there is no correlation (e.g. no liquid proxy available) and becomes less convex if there is correlation. It is linear (see Proposition 4.1) in the limit as the correlation ρ approaches one. Here again, we observe that the

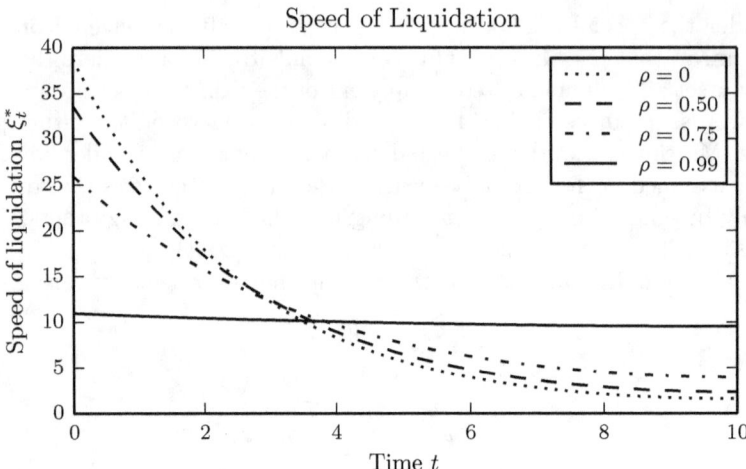

Figure 1: The policy ξ^*, the optimal speed at which shares of the primary asset are liquidated in the no-drift market. Parameters: $\alpha = 10$, $\sigma = \sigma_I = 0.03$, $\theta = 0.05$, $\eta_0 = 100$, $T = 10$.

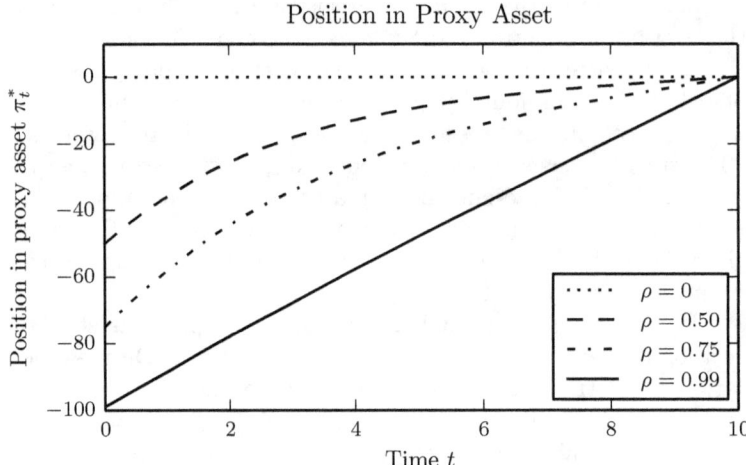

Figure 2: The policy π^*, the optimal number of shares in the proxy asset over time in the no-drift market. Parameters: $\alpha = 10$, $\sigma = \sigma_I = 0.03$, $\theta = 0.05$, $\eta_0 = 100$, $T = 10$.

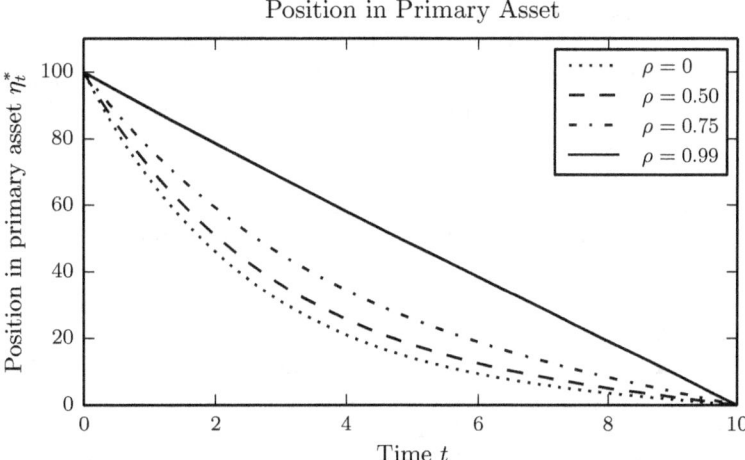

Figure 3: The policy η^*, the optimal number of shares in the primary asset over time in the no-drift market. Parameters: $\alpha = 10$, $\sigma = \sigma_I = 0.03$, $\theta = 0.05$, $\eta_0 = 100$, $T = 10$.

availability of the proxy for use as a hedge allows the investor to be less aggressive in his liquidation strategy.

The following propositions yield various results that hold in the no-drift market.

Proposition 4.1. *If $\mu = \mu_I = 0$, the optimal strategies are given by (21), (22) and (23), where κ_ρ is as in (24). Moreover, the following assertions hold:*

i) The optimal policy ξ_t^* satisfies

$$\lim_{\rho \uparrow 1} \xi_t^* = \frac{\eta_0}{T}, \qquad 0 \leq t \leq T. \tag{25}$$

ii) Let $\xi_t^*(\alpha, \rho)$ and $\eta_t^*(\alpha, \rho)$ denote (22) and (23), respectively, for risk aversion coefficient α and correlation parameter ρ. Then,

$$\xi_t^*(\alpha, \rho) = \xi_t^*(\widehat{\alpha}, \widehat{\rho}) \quad \text{and} \quad \eta_t^*(\alpha, \rho) = \eta_t^*(\widehat{\alpha}, \widehat{\rho}) \tag{26}$$

for all $t \in [0, T]$, if and only if

$$\alpha(1 - \rho^2) = \widehat{\alpha}(1 - \widehat{\rho}^2). \tag{27}$$

iii) Let $\xi_t^*(\theta, \rho)$ and $\eta_t^*(\theta, \rho)$ denote (22) and (23), respectively, for temporary price impact parameter θ and correlation parameter ρ. Then,

$$\xi_t^*(\theta, \rho) = \xi_t^*(\widehat{\theta}, \widehat{\rho}) \quad \text{and} \quad \eta_t^*(\theta, \rho) = \eta_t^*(\widehat{\theta}, \widehat{\rho}) \tag{28}$$

for all $t \in [0, T]$, if and only if

$$\frac{1 - \rho^2}{\theta} = \frac{1 - \widehat{\rho}^2}{\widehat{\theta}}. \tag{29}$$

The above results show how the liquid proxy acts as a hedge on the market risk incurred by liquidating the position in the primary asset over time. Observe that the right-hand side of (25) is the VWAP strategy (10), which is optimal for a risk-neutral investor. That is, the hedge becomes "perfect" as ρ approaches one, in the sense that the investor's optimal strategy is to act as if he is effectively risk-neutral. Note that, although the presence of the proxy asset allows the investor to hedge the market risk involved with liquidating the position in the primary asset over time, it does *not* allow the investor to hedge the price impact risk (represented by the coefficient of temporary price impact θ in (24)).

The effect of the proxy asset on the investor's optimal liquidation strategies is also shown in part (ii) of the above proposition. This result shows explicitly the trade off between the investor's risk aversion and his ability to hedge the market risk in his liquidation. For example, the optimal strategies involving the primary asset for an investor with risk aversion α and proxy asset with correlation ρ are the same as for an investor with no effective hedge available ($\rho = 0$) and risk aversion $\alpha(1-\rho^2)$. In effect, for a fixed risk aversion coefficient, an increase in the correlation between the proxy and (unaffected component of) the primary causes the investor to act *as if* he were less risk-averse. Note that this equivalence of strategies only holds for the investor's position in the primary asset and not for his position in the proxy asset itself (see (21)).

Part (iii) of the above proposition shows a similar result on the effects of the temporary price impact parameter θ and the correlation parameter ρ on the optimal liquidation strategies in the primary asset. The availability of the proxy asset to hedge market risk effectively causes the investor's position in the primary asset to be *as if* the temporary price impact effect were actually lower. In particular, the investor's strategies in the primary asset when there is no proxy with which to effectively hedge the market risk ($\rho = 0$) and the temporary impact is θ are the same as the strategies when there is a hedge available with correlation ρ and the temporary impact is equal to $(1-\rho^2)\theta$.

Proposition 4.2. Let $\mu = \mu_I = 0$. Then, the following assertions hold:
i) The investor's value function (12) at initial time is given by

$$v(T, x_0, \eta_0) = -\exp\left(-\alpha x_0 + \alpha\theta\kappa_\rho \coth(\kappa_\rho T)\eta_0^2\right), \tag{30}$$

where x_0 is as in (7). It is increasing in the correlation ρ.

ii) The broker-dealer's minimum fee at initial time $t = 0$ is given by

$$h(\eta_0, T) = \left(\frac{\gamma}{2} + \theta\kappa_\rho \coth(\kappa_\rho T)\right)\eta_0^2 - S_0^I \eta_0. \tag{31}$$

The above result shows that the investor is better off if he can find a liquid and correlated proxy asset to hedge the market risk incurred by liquidating the primary asset over time. The proposition also yields the broker-dealer's minimum fee (31) in the no-drift market. Observe that both the value function and the indifference price exhibit dependence on the coefficient of permanent price impact γ (through x_0 in (30); see (7)), whereas the optimal liquidation strategies only depend on temporary price impact θ and are independent of permanent price impact.

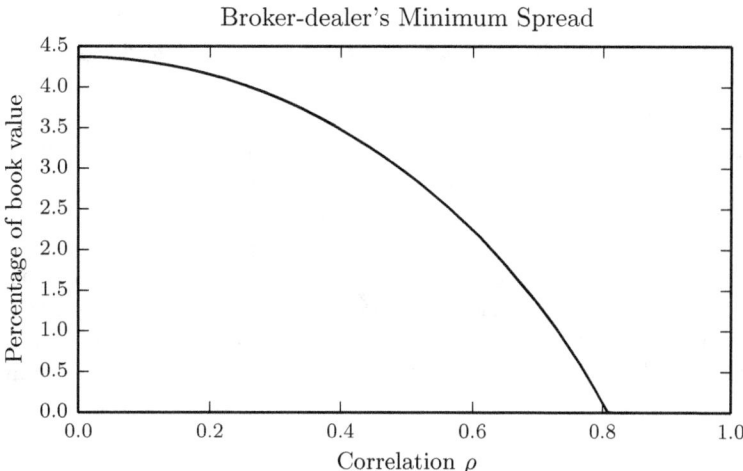

Figure 4: The broker-dealer's minimum spread, the indifference price expressed as a percentage of the initial book value of the primary asset. Parameters: $\alpha = 1$, $\sigma = \sigma_I = 0.019$, $\gamma = 7.5 \times 10^{-5}$, $\theta = 1 \times 10^{-7}$, $\eta_0 = 25,000$, $T = 5$.

Figure 4 depicts the broker-dealer's minimum (percentage) spread or discount to the book value of the position as a function of the correlation ρ. This discount is calculated by dividing the minimum fee $h(\eta_0, T)$ in (31) by $S_0^I \eta_0$, the initial book value of the position. The graph shows that the greater the broker-dealer is able to hedge his market risk, the lower is his minimum spread.

5 Conclusions and possible extensions

This paper studies the problem of an investor who hedges the market risk involved in liquidating a large position in a primary asset over time by simultaneously investing liquidation proceeds in a liquid proxy asset and a money market account. Such a problem is commonly encountered in practice by broker-dealers. In a simple Almgren-Chriss type model, we show that the solution is deterministic if the investor has CARA preferences. We find the optimal strategies explicitly and study their properties. We also explicitly find the broker-dealer's minimum fee it should charge to provide instant liquidity to a financial institution in a block trade on a principal basis. This fee has a natural interpretation as the broker-dealer's indifference price. In the no-drift special case of the model, we provide results on the interplay among risk aversion, price impact risk, and market risk. We find that it is always better, from an expected utility perspective, for the investor to find a relatively liquid proxy asset to hedge market risk in the liquidation of a primary asset.

There are a number of directions for future research. For example, we assume herein that the liquidation must be complete by some exogenous terminal time, which effectively restricts the investor's set of possible strategies. It would be more realistic to consider a problem in which the terminal date for liquidation date is endogenous.[3] We expect that the availability of the proxy would give the investor more time to liquidate.

In addition, the assumption of perfect liquidity of the proxy asset could be relaxed in a more realistic model. Furthermore, one could check the robustness of the results derived herein by considering more general models of price impact and more general utility functions or risk criteria. In particular, while the CARA preferences of the investor implied that his optimal strategies were independent of his initial wealth, we do not expect this to hold for other utility functions.

Finally, one could also consider a more realistic setting in which the investor receives multiple orders that arrive at random times during the liquidation or investment period, or a model in which the investor completes the liquidation and then continues investing.

Appendix

Proof of Theorem 3.1. The proof proceeds in three steps. First, we show the equality

$$\sup_{(\pi,\xi)\in\mathcal{A}(T,\eta_0)} \mathbb{E}[u(X_T^{\pi,\xi})] = \sup_{(\pi,\xi)\in\mathcal{A}_{\det}(T,\eta_0)} \mathbb{E}[u(X_T^{\pi,\xi})], \qquad (32)$$

where u is the exponential utility (11) and $\mathcal{A}_{\det}(T,\eta_0)$ is the subset of deterministic strategies in $\mathcal{A}(T,\eta_0)$. In the second step, we solve the right-hand side of (32), using calculus of variations to find the unique maximizer over deterministic strategies. By the first step, this deterministic strategy also maximizes the expected utility over all strategies. Finally, we observe that the optimal strategy is unique since the mapping $(\pi,\xi) \to \mathbb{E}(u(X_T^{\pi,\xi}))$ is strictly concave.

To begin, we prove (32) by adapting techniques used in Schied et al. (2010). To this end, for $(\pi,\xi) \in \mathcal{A}(T,\eta_0)$, define the processes $Y_t^{\pi,\xi}$ and $Z_t^{\pi,\xi}$, $0 \le t \le T$, by

$$Y_t^{\pi,\xi} = -\alpha\left(\sigma\int_0^t \pi_s dW_s + \sigma_I \int_0^t \eta_s(\rho dW_s + \sqrt{1-\rho^2}dW_s^\perp)\right)$$

and

$$Z_t^{\pi,\xi} = -\alpha\left(\mu\int_0^t \pi_s ds + \mu_I \int_0^t \eta_s ds - \theta\int_0^t \xi_s^2 ds\right),$$

respectively, where $W_t^I = \rho W_t + \sqrt{1-\rho^2}W_t^\perp$ for some Brownian motion $W^\perp$ that is independent of W.

Observe that, since $|\pi_t|$ and $|\xi_t|$ are assumed to be uniformly bounded, the process $Y_t^{\pi,\xi}, 0 \le t \le T$, is a martingale, with $Y_0^{\pi,\xi} = 0$ and its quadratic variation

---

[3]Upon completion of this work, the author became aware of the preprint Bechler and Ludkovski (2014) in which the terminal date for the liquidation is determined endogenously. Endogeneity of the liquidation time, however, requires informational effects from liquidation to be explicitly modeled, unlike in the present paper. Indeed, herein it is easily seen that the value function (12) is strictly increasing in the terminal horizon T.

given by

$$\langle Y^{\pi,\xi}\rangle_t = \alpha^2 \left(\sigma^2 \int_0^t \pi_s^2 dt + 2\rho\sigma\sigma_I \int_0^t \eta_s \pi_s ds + \sigma_I^2 \int_0^t \eta_s^2 ds\right).$$

Now let $\mathcal{E}(Y^{\pi,\xi})_t$, $0 \leq t \leq T$, denote the stochastic exponential, $\mathcal{E}(Y^{\pi,\xi})_t = e^{Y_t^{\pi,\xi} - \frac{1}{2}\langle Y^{\pi,\xi}\rangle_t}$, and observe that $\mathbb{E}[\mathcal{E}(Y^{\pi,\xi})_T] = 1$ by Novikov's condition. Then,

$$\frac{d\mathbb{P}^{\pi,\xi}}{d\mathbb{P}} = \mathcal{E}(Y^{\pi,\xi})_T,$$

defines a measure $\mathbb{P}^{\pi,\xi}$ on $\mathcal{F}_T$ that is equivalent to $\mathbb{P}$.

Next, we define

$$m := \inf_{(\pi,\xi)\in\mathcal{A}_{\det}(T,\eta_0)} \left[\frac{1}{2}\langle Y^{\pi,\xi}\rangle_t + Z_T^{\pi,\xi}\right].$$

It is easily seen that (32) follows trivially if $m = -\infty$. If $m > -\infty$, then we have, for all $(\pi,\xi) \in \mathcal{A}(T,\eta_0)$, that

$$m \leq \frac{1}{2}\langle Y^{\pi,\xi}\rangle_t + Z_T^{\pi,\xi}, \qquad \mathbb{P}-a.s.$$

Let $\varepsilon > 0$ and find $(\pi^\varepsilon,\xi^\varepsilon) \in \mathcal{A}_{\det}(T,\eta_0)$ such that

$$\frac{1}{2}\langle Y^{\pi^\varepsilon,\xi^\varepsilon}\rangle_t + Z_T^{\pi^\varepsilon,\xi^\varepsilon} \leq m + \varepsilon.$$

Then, for all $(\pi,\xi) \in \mathcal{A}(T,\eta_0)$,

$$\begin{aligned}
\mathbb{E}[u(X_T^{\pi,\xi})] &= -e^{-\alpha x_0}\mathbb{E}\left[e^{Y_T^{\pi,\xi}+Z_T^{\pi,\xi}}\right] \\
&= -e^{-\alpha x_0}\mathbb{E}\left[e^{Y_T^{\pi,\xi}-\frac{1}{2}\langle Y^{\pi,\xi}\rangle_T+\frac{1}{2}\langle Y^{\pi,\xi}\rangle_T+Z_T^{\pi,\xi}}\right] \\
&= -e^{-\alpha x_0}\mathbb{E}^{\pi,\xi}\left[e^{\frac{1}{2}\langle Y^{\pi,\xi}\rangle_T+Z_T^{\pi,\xi}}\right] \\
&\leq -e^{-\varepsilon}e^{-\alpha x_0}\mathbb{E}^{\pi,\xi}\left[e^{\frac{1}{2}\langle Y^{\pi^\varepsilon,\xi^\varepsilon}\rangle_T+Z_T^{\pi^\varepsilon,\xi^\varepsilon}}\right] \\
&= -e^{-\varepsilon}e^{-\alpha x_0+\frac{1}{2}\langle Y^{\pi^\varepsilon,\xi^\varepsilon}\rangle_T+Z_T^{\pi^\varepsilon,\xi^\varepsilon}} \\
&= -e^{-\varepsilon}\mathbb{E}\left[u(X_T^{\pi^\varepsilon,\xi^\varepsilon})\right],
\end{aligned}$$

where $\mathbb{E}^{\pi,\xi}$ denotes expectation under the measure $\mathbb{P}^{\pi,\xi}$. It follows easily that

$$\sup_{(\pi,\xi)\in\mathcal{A}(T,\eta_0)} \mathbb{E}[u(X_T^{\pi,\xi})] \leq e^{-\varepsilon}\mathbb{E}[u(X_T^{\pi^\varepsilon,\xi^\varepsilon})] \leq e^{-\varepsilon}\sup_{(\pi,\xi)\in\mathcal{A}_{\det}(T,\eta_0)} \mathbb{E}[u(X_T^{\pi,\xi})].$$

Finally, letting $\varepsilon \downarrow 0$ yields

$$\sup_{(\pi,\xi)\in\mathcal{A}(T,\eta_0)} \mathbb{E}[u(X_T^{\pi,\xi})] \leq \sup_{(\pi,\xi)\in\mathcal{A}_{\det}(T,\eta_0)} \mathbb{E}[u(X_T^{\pi,\xi})].$$

Using that the opposite inequality clearly holds, the proof of (32) is complete.

Having shown (32), we now specify the optimal deterministic policy. First note that optimizing

$$\mathbb{E}[u(X_T^{\pi,\xi})] = -\exp\left(-\alpha x_0 - \alpha \left(\mu_I \int_0^T \eta_t dt + \mu \int_0^T \pi_t dt - \theta \int_0^T \dot\xi_t^2 dt \right.\right.$$
$$\left.\left. - \frac{\alpha}{2}\left(\sigma^2 \int_0^T \pi_t^2 dt + 2\rho\sigma\sigma_I \int_0^T \eta_t \pi_t dt + \sigma_I^2 \int_0^T \eta_t^2 dt\right)\right)\right) \quad (33)$$

over deterministic strategies is equivalent to minimizing the functional

$$\int_0^T F(t, y(t), y'(t))dt, \qquad y(t) = (\pi_t, \eta_t), \quad (34)$$

over curves $y(t)$ with $y(0) = (0, \eta_0)$ and $y(T)$ having second coordinate equal to 0 (i.e. $\eta_T = 0$), where F is given by

$$F(t, y, z) := \frac{\alpha}{2} y^\top \Sigma y - b^\top y + z^\top L z, \qquad y, z \in \mathbb{R}^2,$$

and the quantities Σ, b and L are defined by

$$\Sigma := \begin{pmatrix} \sigma^2 & \rho\sigma\sigma_I \\ \rho\sigma\sigma_I & \sigma_I^2 \end{pmatrix}, \quad b := \begin{pmatrix} \mu \\ \mu_I \end{pmatrix}, \quad L := \begin{pmatrix} 0 & 0 \\ 0 & \theta \end{pmatrix}.$$

Next, we consider the mapping $G\colon (y,z) \mapsto F(t,y,z)$. Then, G has Hessian $D^2 G = \alpha \Sigma + 2L$, which is easily seen to be positive definite. The map G is thus strictly convex, and results from calculus of variations (see, for example, Touzi (2010), Theorem 2.10) imply that the unique minimizer to (34) is the solution to the Euler-Lagrange equation

$$\alpha \Sigma y(t) = b + 2L y''(t).$$

This, in turn, can be written in components as the set of equations

$$\begin{cases} \sigma^2 \pi_t + \rho\sigma\sigma_I \eta_t = \dfrac{\mu}{\alpha} \\ \rho\sigma\sigma_I \pi_t + \sigma_I^2 \eta_t = \dfrac{\mu_I}{\alpha} + \dfrac{2\theta}{\alpha}\ddot\eta_t. \end{cases} \quad (35)$$

Substituting the first equation into the second, we obtain the following second-order linear inhomogeneous ordinary differential equation (ODE) for η_t,

$$2\theta \ddot\eta_t - (1-\rho^2)\alpha\sigma_I^2 \eta_t = \frac{\mu}{\sigma}\rho\sigma_I - \mu_I, \quad (36)$$

subject to the initial and terminal conditions

$$\eta_0 = \eta_0 > 0, \qquad \eta_T = 0.$$

Finally, the ODE (36) is solved by (16), where κ_ρ is as in (13). We find (14) using (35), and (15) upon differentiating (16). □

Proof of Proposition 3.2. If the investor does not trade, then his value function in (12) is given by $v(T,0,0) = u(0) = -1$. Otherwise, if he does trade, then $v(T,x_0,\eta_0)$ is equal to (18). The indifference price $h(\eta_0,T)$ satisfies

$$-1 = u(0) = v(T, x_0 + h(\eta_0,T), \eta_0),$$

where x_0 is as in (7). We then deduce (19), using (18). □

Proof of Proposition 4.1. Part i) follows by an application of l'Hôspital's rule to (22). For parts ii) and iii), observe first that (22) and (23) depend on the parameters α, ρ and θ only through κ_ρ. The results then follow immediately upon examining κ_ρ in (24). □

Proof of Proposition 4.2. Part i) follows from (18) and the identities

$$\int_0^T (\xi_t^*)^2 dt = \frac{\alpha \sigma_I^2(1-\rho^2)}{2\theta} \frac{\eta_0^2}{\sinh^2(\kappa_\rho T)} \left(\frac{T}{2} + \frac{\sinh(2\kappa_\rho T)}{4\kappa_\rho} \right)$$

and

$$\int_0^T (\eta_t^*)^2 dt = \frac{\eta_0^2}{\sinh^2(\kappa_\rho T)} \left(\frac{\sinh(2\kappa_\rho T)}{4\kappa_\rho} - \frac{T}{2} \right).$$

Differentiating (30), we easily obtain that the value function is increasing in ρ. Part ii) follows from i) and the equality $v(T, x_0 + h(\eta_0,T), \eta_0) = -1$, with x_0 is as in (7). □

References

A. Alfonsi, A. Schied, and A. Slynko. Order book resilience, price manipulation, and the positive portfolio problem. *SIAM Journal of Financial Mathematics*, 3 (1):511–533, 2012.

R. Almgren. Optimal execution with nonlinear impact functions and trading-enhanced risk. *Applied Mathematical Finance*, 10(1):1–18, 2003.

R. Almgren and N. Chriss. Value under liquidation. *Risk*, 12:61–63, 1999.

R. Almgren and N. Chriss. Optimal execution of portfolio transactions. *Journal of Risk*, 3:5–39, 2001.

R. Almgren, C. Thum, E. Hauptmann, and H. Li. Equity market impact. *Risk*, 18 (7):57–62, 2005.

S. Ankirchner, P. Kratz, and T. Kruse. Hedging forward positions: basis risk versus liquidity costs. Working paper, June 2013. Available at SSRN: http://ssrn.com/abstract=2100768.

K. Bechler and M. Ludkovski. Optimal execution with dynamic order flow imbalance. Available at arxiv.org/abs/1409.2618, September 2014.

D. Bertsimas and A. Lo. Optimal control of execution costs. *Journal of Financial Markets*, 1(1):1–50, 1998.

K. Burdett and M. O'Hara. Building blocks: An introduction to block trading. *Journal of Banking and Finance*, 11(2):193–212, 1987.

D. Easley and M. O'Hara. Price, trade size, and information in securities markets. *Journal of Financial Economics*, 19(1):69–90, 1987.

A. Frino, D. Gallagher, and T. Oetomo. Further analysis of the liquidity and information components of institutional orders: Active versus passive funds. *Pacific-Basin Finance Journal*, 14(5):439–452, 2006.

K. Froot and J. Stein. Risk management, capital budgeting and capital structure policy for financial institutions: An integrated approach. *Journal of Financial Economics*, 47(1):55–82, 1998.

J. Gatheral and A. Schied. Optimal trade execution under geometric Brownian motion in the Almgren and Chriss framework. *International Journal of Theoretical and Applied Finance*, 14(3):353–368, 2011.

S. Grossman and M. Miller. Liquidity and market structure. *Journal of Finance*, 43(3):617–633, 1988.

R. Holthausen, R. Leftwich, and D. Mayers. The effect of large block transactions on security prices: A cross-sectional analysis. *Journal of Financial Economics*, 19(2):237–267, 1987.

R. Holthausen, R. Leftwich, and D. Mayers. Large-block transactions, the speed of response, and temporary and permanent stock-price effects. *Journal of Financial Economics*, 26(1):71–95, 1990.

G. Huberman and W. Stanzl. Price manipulation and quasi-arbitrage. *Econometrica*, 72(4):1247–1275, 2004.

D. Keim and A. Madhavan. The upstairs market for large-block transactions: Analysis and measurement of price effects. *Review of Financial Studies*, 9(1):1–36, 1995a.

D. Keim and A. Madhavan. Execution costs and investment performance: An empirical analysis of institutional equity trades. Rodney L. White Center Working Paper No. 26-94, The Wharton School, The University of Pennsylvania, 1995b.

F. Klöck, A. Schied, and Y. Sun. Price manipulation in a market impact model with dark pool. Working paper, 2011. Available at SSRN: http://ssrn.com/abstract=1785409.

A. Kraus and H. Stoll. Price impacts of block trading on the New York Stock Exchange. *Journal of Finance*, 27(3):569–588, 1972.

A. Kyle. Continuous auctions and insider trading. *Econometrica*, 53(6):1315–1335, 1985.

T. Li and R. Almgren. A fully-dynamic closed-form solution for delta-hedging with market impact. Working paper, 2014. Available at http://www.courant.nyu.edu/~almgren/pubs.html.

A. Madhavan. Market microstructure: A survey. *Journal of Financial Markets*, 3(3):205–258, 2000.

R. Merton. Lifetime portfolio selection under uncertainty: The continuous-time case. *The Review of Economics and Statistics*, 51(3):247–257, 1969.

A. Obizhaeva. Information vs. liquidity: Evidence from portfolio transition trades. Working paper, 2007. Available at SSRN: http://ssrn.com/abstract=965743.

A. Obizhaeva and J. Wang. Optimal trading strategy and supply/demand dynamics. *Journal of Financial Markets*, 16(1):1–32, 2013.

S. Predoiu, G. Shaikhet, and S. Shreve. Optimal execution in a general one-sided limit-order book. *SIAM Journal of Financial Mathematics*, 2(1):183–212, 2011.

A. Roch and H. Soner. Resilient price impact of trading and the cost of illiquidity. *International Journal of Theoretical and Applied Finance*, 16(6), 2013.

L. Rogers and S. Singh. The cost of illiquidity and its effects on hedging. *Mathematical Finance*, 20(4):597–615, 2010.

D. Ryu. Price impact asymmetry of futures trades: Trade direction and trade size. *Emerging Markets Review*, 14:110–130, 2013.

A. Schied. Robust strategies for optimal order execution in the Almgren-Chriss framework. *Applied Mathematical Finance*, 20(3):264–286, 2013.

A. Schied and T. Schöneborn. Risk aversion and the dynamics of optimal liquidation strategies in illiquid markets. *Finance and Stochastics*, 13(2):181–204, 2009.

A. Schied, T. Schöneborn, and M. Tehranchi. Optimal basket liquidation for CARA investors is deterministic. *Applied Mathematical Finance*, 17(6):471–489, 2010.

T. Schöneborn. Trade execution in illiquid markets. Optimal control and multi-agent equilibrium. Doctoral dissertation, TU Berlin, 2008.

D. Seppi. Equilibrium block trading and asymmetric information. *Journal of Finance*, 45(1):73–94, 1990.

H. Stoll. The supply of dealer services in security markets. *Journal of Finance*, 33(4):1133–1151, 1978.

H. Stoll. Inferring the components of the bid-ask spread: Theory and empirical evidence. *Journal of Finance*, 44(1):115–134, 1989.

N. Touzi. Deterministic and stochastic control. Application to finance. Lecture notes, 2010. Available at http://www.cmap.polytechnique.fr/~touzi/Master-LN.pdf.

www.ingramcontent.com/pod-product-compliance
Lightning Source LLC
Chambersburg PA
CBHW081823170526
45167CB00008B/3526